Colourful Creatures

Nicholas Brasch

Contents

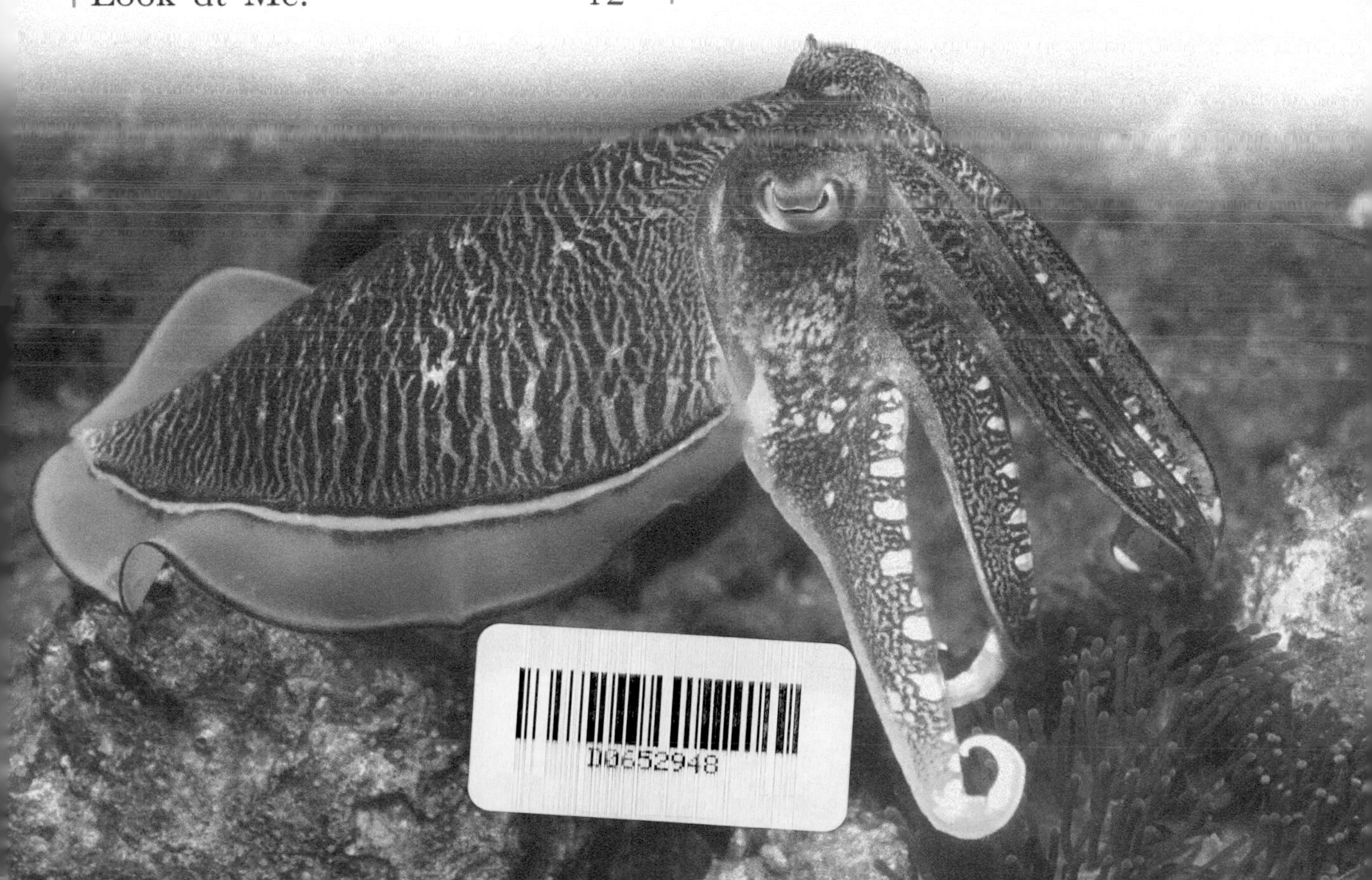

Meet Tessa

Hi, I'm Tessa. I take photos of animals.

An animal's colour can help it do different things. Come on – I'll show you!

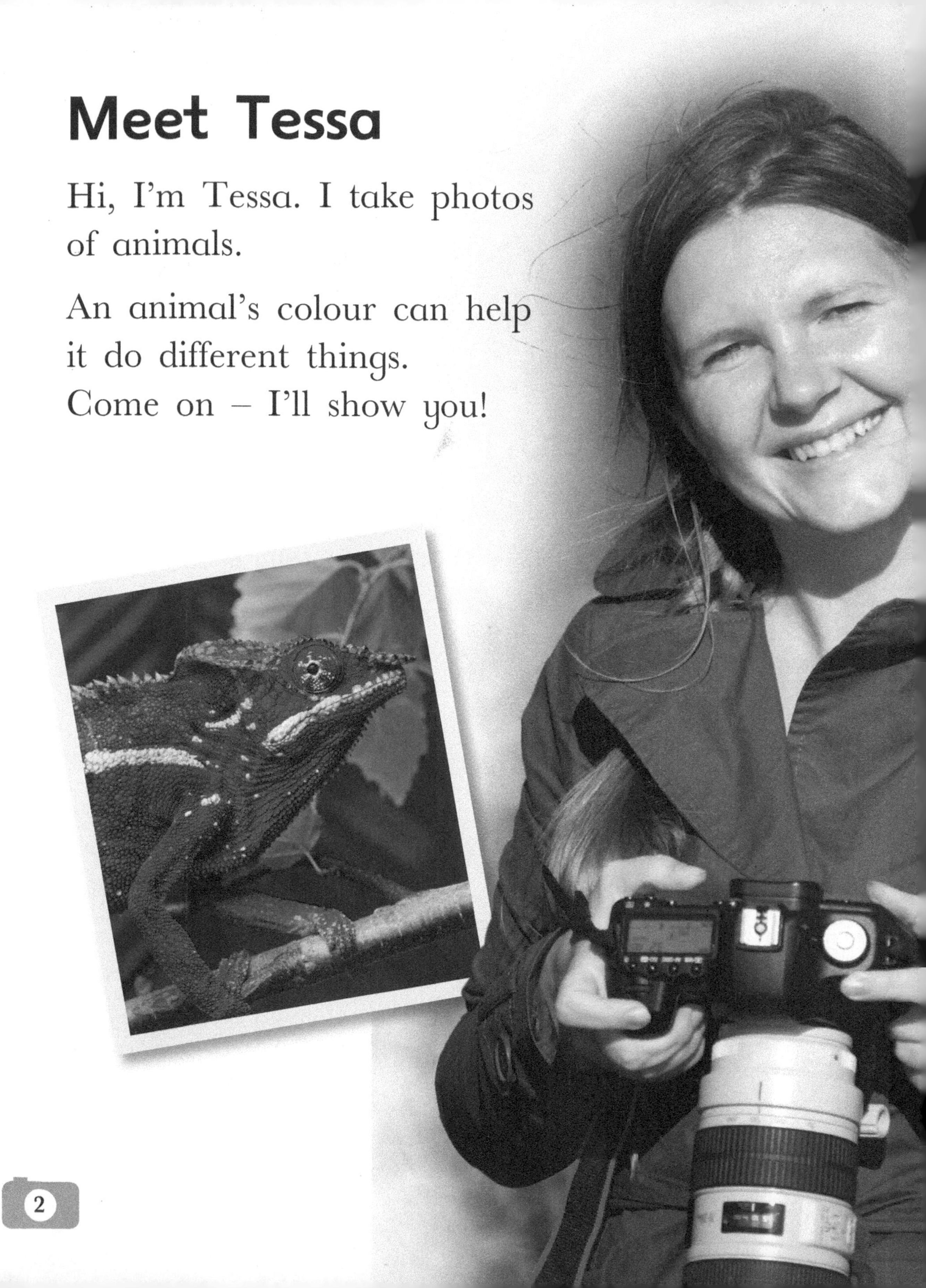

Don't Eat Me!

Some animals use colour to stop other animals eating them.

Common Tiger butterfly

Tiger Butterfly

Birds eat butterflies, but not the Tiger butterfly!

Its black and orange colour makes birds think that it will taste really bad!

Just Like Me!

This butterfly looks just like the Tiger butterfly. It has the same colours. Birds think it will also taste bad!

Leopard Lacewing butterfly

Tiger butterfly

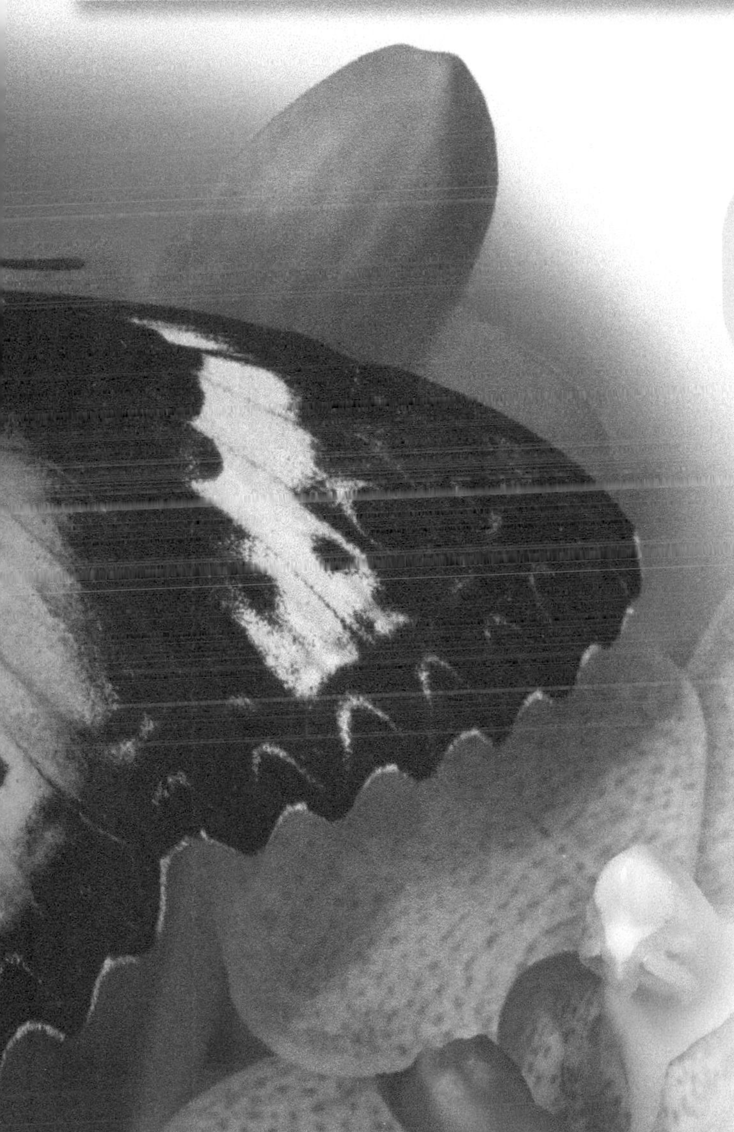

Can you spot the differences?

A Tricky Hunter

Some animals use colour to trick other animals.

Tiger

The tiger has orange fur with black stripes.

The tiger uses **camouflage** (say: *cam-oh-flarj*) to help it hunt. Its colour helps it to hide in long grass. Other animals cannot see it coming!

I'm Watching You!

Tigers have white spots on the backs of their ears. These spots look like eyes. They are called '**eye-spots**'!

The spots trick other animals into thinking the tiger is looking at them!

Eye-spots

Some butterflies have eye-spots to scare away other animals too.

Look at Me!

Many animals use colour to find a **mate**.

Peacocks

Peacocks have bright blue and green feathers on their tails. The feathers have spots that look like eyes.

Male and Female

Males are called peacocks.
Females are called peahens.

When a peacock sees a peahen, he opens up his tail feathers. This makes the peahen look at him.

Colourful Changes

Some animals can change colour!

Cuttlefish

Cuttlefish change colour to hide from sharks, dolphins and other cuttlefish who want to eat them.

Cuttlefish can use camouflage to match the colour of what is around them.

This cuttlefish is brown, like the sand.

This cuttlefish is red, like the rocks.

Chameleon

The chameleon is a type of lizard (say: *ca-meel-i-an*).

Different chameleons can change into different colours:

- pink
- green
- blue
- red
- black
- yellow!

Chameleons change colour to camouflage themselves to find mates. A male chameleon will show a bright colour to find a female.

A Colour Battle!

Male chameleons sometimes have a colour battle! The winner is the one with the brightest colour.

More Colourful Creatures

How do these animals use colour? Try this quiz!

Glossary

camouflage
colours that help animals hide from other animals, and also attract a mate

eye-spots
coloured spots on an animal that look like eyes

mate
when a male and female become partners

male
men or boys

female
women or girls

Index

Quiz Answers

1. To find a mate

2. As camouflage to hide in the long grass from animals which hunt them

3. To tell other animals to keep away